Sanjeev Kapoor

Vegetarian

After-School Snacks

In association with Alyona Kapoor

Popular Prakashan
www.popularprakashan.com

Published by
POPULAR PRAKASHAN PVT. LTD.
301, Mahalaxmi Chambers
22, Bhulabhai Desai Road
Mumbai - 400 026
for Khana Khazana Publications Pvt. Ltd.

First Published 2010
Third Reprint 2014

(4096)
ISBN: 978-81-7991-348-2

Design: Anjali Sawant
Photography: Alim Bolar, Bharat Bhirangi & Swapnil Naik

PRINTED IN INDIA
by Saurabh Printers Pvt. Ltd.
A-16, Sector 4, Noida

Author's Note

Kids today need all the nutrition they can get! Be it a pre-teen or teenager, a growing kid today is always on the go: from school to home for a quick snack and then off to tuitions, sports, and to chill out with friends!

Knowing they are picky about what they eat, and their love for junk food, how does one feed them something delicious and nutritious at the same time?

Here is my answer: a selection of mouth-watering recipes that will definitely have famished kids of all ages eagerly looking forward to yummy home-made after-school snacks. Snacks which will both satisfy their hunger and give them the boost of energy they need for their activity-filled lives. Your kids will love the delicious Mini Falafel Burgers, and the sweetly-satisfying, energy-giving treats such as Peanut Raisin Bars. Snacks like Cajun Vegetable Pizza and Singapore Noodles will be the perfect answer to their craving for something appetising and substantial.

Happy cooking!

Contents

Chana Puri

¾ cup split Bengal gram, soaked overnight

1 inch ginger

2-3 garlic cloves

Salt to taste

1 tablespoon coriander powder

1 tablespoon cumin powder

1 teaspoon red chilli powder

¼ teaspoon turmeric powder

¼ teaspoon dried mango powder

1 tablespoon cumin seeds

½ tablespoon dried pomegranate seeds

1½ tablespoons oil

2 green chillies, slit

1 medium tomato, quartered

½ teaspoon *garam masala* powder

Puri

1 cup wholewheat flour

2 tablespoons semolina

Salt to taste

Oil for deep-frying

Chana Puri

- Pound the ginger and garlic to a fine paste.
- Drain the split Bengal gram, add two and half cups of water and salt and cook till tender. Drain and reserve the cooking liquid.
- Mix together the coriander, cumin, chilli, turmeric and dried mango powders. Dry-roast the cumin seeds and dried pomegranate seeds separately. Cool and grind the seeds together to a powder. Mix together with the rest of the spice powders.
- Heat one tablespoon of oil in a non-stick *kadai*. Add the green chillies and ginger-garlic paste and stir-fry for a few seconds. Add the mixed spice powder and stir-fry for half a minute. Stir in one-fourth cup of the reserved cooking liquid and cook for two minutes.
- Add the cooked gram, salt, half a cup of the reserved cooking liquid and cook on high heat for three to four minutes, stirring occasionally.
- Add the tomato and sprinkle *garam masala* powder and roasted pomegranate seed-cumin seed powder.

- Heat the remaining oil and pour over the prepared gram. Stir well and adjust the seasoning.
- For the *puri*, knead the flour and semolina with salt and enough water to make a semi-soft dough. Cover with a damp cloth and rest the dough for half an hour.
- Divide the dough into twelve equal portions and roll out each portion into a *puri*.
- Heat sufficient oil in a non-stick *kadai* and deep-fry the *puri* on medium heat till golden. Drain on absorbent paper.
- Serve hot with the *chana*.

Aloo Paneer Rolls

2 large potatoes, boiled and mashed

200 grams cottage cheese, grated

1 tablespoon oil + for deep-frying

1 medium onion, chopped

½ tablespoon chilli flakes

3-4 green chillies, chopped

4 tablespoons chopped fresh coriander

1 teaspoon *garam masala* powder

Salt to taste

1 tablespoon raisins, soaked

4 tablespoons refined flour

Black pepper powder to taste

½ cup milk

1 cup breadcrumbs

- Heat one tablespoon of oil in a non-stick frying pan and sauté the onion till translucent.
- Mix together the potatoes, cottage cheese, fried onion, chilli flakes, green chillies, chopped coriander, *garam masala* powder, salt and raisins. Shape the mixture into cylindrical croquettes.

- Season the flour with the salt and pepper powder. Roll the croquettes in the flour, then dip in the milk and roll in the breadcrumbs. Place the croquettes in the refrigerator for an hour or more to chill.
- Heat sufficient oil in a non-stick *kadai* and deep-fry the rolls till golden brown. Drain on absorbent paper.
- Serve hot with Green Chutney (page 93).

Chef's Tips

- Fry one croquette to start with to check if the mixture binds together and whether the oil is sufficiently hot.
- Make sure that you don't put the boiled potatoes into cold water to cool. They will become soggy.

Besan Cheela With Methi-Cheese Stuffing

2 cups gram flour

1 cup chopped fresh fenugreek leaves

2½ cups cottage cheese, grated

1 tablespoon oil + for shallow-frying

2 medium onions, chopped

8-10 fresh button mushrooms, sliced

Salt to taste

¼ teaspoon black pepper powder

¼ teaspoon soda bicarbonate

1 teaspoon red chilli powder

1 teaspoon carom seeds

A pinch of asafoetida

2 tablespoons chopped fresh coriander

- Heat one tablespoon of oil in a non-stick pan and sauté the onions till translucent. Add the chopped fenugreek and cook for another minute. Add the mushrooms and sauté on high heat for a minute. Add the salt and pepper powder, and remove from heat. Leave to cool and mix in the cottage cheese. Set aside.

Besan Cheela with Methi-Cheese Stuffing

- In a bowl, mix together the gram flour, soda bicarbonate, salt, chilli powder, carom seeds, asafoetida, chopped coriander and sufficient water to make a smooth batter of pouring consistency.
- Heat another non-stick pan; drizzle a few drops of oil, pour a ladleful of batter into the pan and spread it evenly and thinly, using the back of the ladle. Cook the *cheela* on both sides, using a little more oil, till golden brown.
- Place a portion of the stuffing on one side of the *cheela*, fold the other side over it and serve immediately.

Boote Ke Samose

4 tablespoons whole green gram, soaked

2½ cups refined flour

3 tablespoons oil + for deep-frying

2 teaspoons green chilli paste, or to taste

Salt to taste

1 tablespoon lemon juice

- Add two tablespoons of oil and half a cup of water to the refined flour and knead to make a moderately firm dough. Cover with a damp cloth and set aside for thirty minutes.
- Heat one tablespoon of oil in a non-stick pan; add the green chilli paste and sauté for two minutes. Add the green gram, salt and half a cup, or just enough water, to cook the gram. Cover and cook till dry. Sauté the mixture for three or four minutes. Stir in the lemon juice.
- Divide the dough into four equal portions and roll each portion out into an elongated *puri*. Cut each *puri* in half and shape each half into a cone. Stuff the cones with the green gram mixture and seal the edges with a little water.

- Heat the oil in a non-stick *kadai* and deep-fry the *samose* till crisp and golden. Drain on absorbent paper.
- Serve hot with Date and Tamarind Chutney (page 93)

Boote ke Samose

Cabbage Rolls

8 cabbage leaves

4 medium potatoes, boiled and mashed

½ cup shelled green peas, boiled and mashed

Salt to taste

1 teaspoon *chaat masala*

1 cup gram flour

½ teaspoon red chilli powder

½ teaspoon soda bicarbonate

Oil for deep-frying

- Blanch the cabbage leaves in boiling salted water. Drain and pat dry with absorbent paper.
- Mix the potatoes, green peas, salt and *chaat masala* in a bowl. Divide the mixture into eight equal portions.
- Place each portion of the mixture at one end of each cabbage leaf. Fold the sides around the filling and roll up the leaves firmly.
- Make a batter of coating consistency with the gram flour, chilli powder, salt, soda bicarbonate and some water.
- Heat sufficient oil in a non-stick *kadai*. Dip the cabbage rolls in the batter and deep-fry until golden brown. Drain on absorbent paper.
- Serve hot with tomato ketchup or Mint Chutney (page 93).

Chinese Dosa

2 cups ready-made *dosa* batter

Oil as required

Filling

2 teaspoons oil

5-6 garlic cloves, chopped

½ medium green capsicum, cut into thin strips

½ medium yellow capsicum, cut into thin strips

½ medium red capsicum, cut into thin strips

1 cup boiled eggless noodles

½ teaspoon soy sauce

1 teaspoon red chilli sauce

2 tablespoons tomato ketchup

Salt to taste

Black pepper powder to taste

2 spring onions with greens, chopped

- To make the filling, heat the oil in a non-stick pan. Add the garlic and sauté for half a minute. Add all the capsicums and sauté for a couple of minutes.
- Add the noodles, soy sauce, chilli sauce and tomato ketchup, and toss to mix. Add the salt and pepper powder, and toss again. Sprinkle the spring onions with greens and mix again. Set aside.
- Heat a non-stick *dosa tawa*, season with oil and wipe with a wet cloth.
- Pour a ladleful of the *dosa* batter on the *tawa* and spread it in a circular motion with the back of the ladle. Drizzle the oil all around and cook for a minute.
- Place a small portion of the filling on one half of the *dosa*. Fold the other half over and press down lightly. Serve hot.

Green Chana Chaat

1½ cups dried green Bengal gram, soaked overnight

1 teaspoon *chaat masala*

2 medium onions, chopped

2 medium tomatoes, chopped

2-3 green chillies, chopped

2 tablespoons chopped fresh coriander

Black salt to taste

1 teaspoon roasted cumin powder

½ teaspoon red chilli powder

2 tablespoons lemon juice

- Pressure-cook the soaked gram in three cups of water till the pressure is released two or three times (two or three whistles), or till tender.
- Transfer the gram to a non-stick *kadai* and simmer till all the water evaporates.
- Place the hot gram in a bowl. Add the onions, tomatoes, green chillies, chopped coriander, black salt, roasted cumin powder, *chaat masala*, chilli powder and lemon juice, and mix well.
- Serve immediately.

Green Chana Chaat

Crunchy Paneer Pakore

250 grams cottage cheese

Oil for deep-frying

1 cup *boondi*

Garlic Chutney

8-10 garlic cloves

1 teaspoon oil

2 teaspoons red chilli powder

Salt to taste

Batter

1 cup gram flour

1½ inches ginger

5 garlic cloves

½ teaspoon red chilli powder

½ teaspoon turmeric powder

A pinch of soda bicarbonate

Salt to taste

- Wash and cut the cottage cheese into two-inch by half-inch by half-inch pieces. Slit each piece in half without cutting through.
- Crush the *boondi* with your hand and set aside.

- To make the garlic chutney, peel and roast the garlic in one teaspoon of oil. Mix with the red chilli powder and salt, and grind to a smooth paste.
- To prepare the batter, grind together the ginger and garlic to make a paste. Mix the gram flour with the paste, chilli powder, turmeric powder, soda bicarbonate and salt. Add sufficient water and whisk well to make a batter of coating consistency. Rest the batter for about fifteen minutes.
- Stuff the garlic chutney into the slit of each cottage cheese piece.
- Heat sufficient oil in a non-stick *kadai*, dip each piece of cottage cheese into the batter, roll in the crushed *boondi* and deep-fry on medium heat till crisp and golden brown.
- Serve hot with tomato ketchup or Green Chutney (page 93).

Pav Bhaji Buns

8 wholewheat *pav*

3 medium tomatoes, chopped

1 medium green capsicum, chopped

¼ cup shelled green peas, blanched and mashed

4 medium potatoes, boiled and grated

3 tablespoons butt[illegible] for shallow-frying

2 tablespoons oil

2 medium onions, chopped

1 green chilli, chopped

1 tablespoon ginger-garlic paste

1½ tablespoons *pav bhaji masala*
Salt to taste
1 tablespoon chopped fresh coriander
1 tablespoon lemon juice

- Heat two tablespoons of butter and the oil in a non-stick pan; add three-fourth of the onions and sauté till light golden brown. Add the green chilli and ginger-garlic paste, and sauté for half a minute.
- Add half the tomatoes and cook on medium heat, stirring continuously, for three to four minutes, or till the oil separates from the *masala*.
- Add the capsicum, green peas, potatoes and one cup of water. Bring to a boil and simmer for ten minutes, pressing down with the back of the spoon a few times, till all the vegetables are completely mashed.
- Add the *pav bhaji masala*, salt and the remaining tomatoes. Cook on medium heat, stirring continuously for two minutes or till the mixture is thick and of spreading consistency. Add the chopped coriander, lemon juice and one tablespoon of butter and remove from heat. Set aside to cool slightly.

- Slit the *pav* without cutting through. Spread some of the vegetable mixture on the lower half and sprinkle some of the remaining onions. Spread some butter on both the outer surfaces of the *pav*.
- Heat a flat non-stick *tawa* and cook the *pav* on low heat till golden and crisp on the outside. Serve hot.

Instant Uttappam

1 cup fine semolina

1 cup yogurt

Salt to taste

¼ teaspoon soda bicarbonate

1 medium onion, chopped

1 medium green capsicum, seeded and chopped

Red chilli powder, to taste

Crushed roasted cumin seeds, to taste

Oil for shallow-frying

- Place the semolina in a bowl with yogurt and salt. Mix well and set aside for fifteen minutes. Add half a cup of water and soda bicarbonate, and mix again.
- Heat a non-stick *tawa* and pour a ladleful of batter in the centre. Do not spread the batter. Sprinkle the onion, capsicum, chilli powder and cumin seeds over the *uttappam*.
- Drizzle half a teaspoon oil around the *uttappam* and cook on moderate heat.
- When the underside has cooked, flip over and drizzle half a teaspoon of oil around and cook the other side till set. Serve hot.

Green Pea And Carrot Dalia

½ cup shelled green peas

2 small carrots, diced

1 cup broken wheat

1 tablespoon oil

1 teaspoon cumin seeds

1 small onion, chopped

1 medium tomato, seeded and chopped

Salt to taste

2 teaspoons butter

2 tablespoons chopped fresh coriander

- Soak the broken wheat in two cups of water for thirty minutes. Drain.
- Heat the oil in a deep non-stick pan and add the cumin seeds. As they begin to change colour, add the onion and sauté till translucent; add the green peas, carrots and tomato, and sauté for one minute.
- Add the broken wheat, three cups of water and salt to taste.
- Bring the mixture to a boil, cover and cook till tender.
- Stir in the butter and chopped coriander, and serve at once.

Green Pea and Carrot Dalia

Handvo

- 1 cup rice
- ½ cup split pigeon peas
- ¼ cup split green gram
- 2 tablespoons split Bengal gram
- 2 tablespoons split black gram
- ½ cup sour yogurt
- 2 teaspoons soda bicarbonate
- Salt to taste
- 4 teaspoons sugar
- 2 teaspoons red chilli powder
- ½ teaspoon turmeric powder
- 1 medium carrot, grated
- ½ cup shelled green peas, boiled
- 5 tablespoons oil
- 2 dried red chillies
- 2 cloves
- 1 bay leaf
- A pinch of asafoetida
- 2 teaspoons mustard seeds
- 1 tablespoon lemon juice
- 3 tablespoons toasted sesame seeds

- Soak the rice together with the split pigeon peas, split green gram, split Bengal gram, and split black gram in five cups of water for two hours. Drain and grind to a coarse paste. Add enough water to make a batter of medium thick consistency. Mix in the yogurt and one teaspoon of soda bicarbonate. Cover the batter and leave to stand in a dark place for two or three hours to ferment.
- Stir the salt, sugar, chilli powder and turmeric powder into the batter. Mix in the grated carrot and green peas.
- Heat the oil in a non-stick pan; add the red chillies, cloves, bay leaf, asafoetida and mustard seeds, and sauté till the seeds begin to splutter.
- Sprinkle the remaining soda bicarbonate over the batter and pour the lemon juice into it. Immediately, pour the hot spices into the batter and whisk briskly.
- Grease a ring mould. Pour the batter into it till half full. Sprinkle the toasted sesame seeds generously over the top.

- Place about two kilograms of clean sand in a large pressure cooker. Place the ring mould in the sand carefully, pressing down till it is embedded about half way into the sand. Cover the cooker with the lid but without the gasket and whistle.
- Cook over high heat for ten minutes. Lower heat to medium and cook the *handvo* till a skewer inserted into it comes out clean. It may take forty to forty-five minutes.
- Cool slightly and unmould the *handvo*. Cut into thick slices and serve hot with Green Chutney (page 93).

Handvo

Khasta Aloo Chaat

4 large potatoes, boiled and mashed

1 teaspoon *chaat masala*

Salt to taste

2 tablespoons cornflour

½ cup thick Green Chutney (page 93)

4-5 tablespoons arrowroot flour

Oil for deep-frying

1 tablespoon Red Chilli-Garlic Chutney (page 94)

4-5 tablespoons Date and Tamarind Chutney (page 93)

- In a large bowl, combine the potatoes with salt and cornflour, and mix well. Divide the potato mixture into sixteen equal portions and shape into lemon-sized balls.
- Flatten a portion of the mashed potato on your palm and place one teaspoon of the green chutney in the centre. Bring the sides together to enclose the filling and shape into small squares. Dust with a little arrowroot flour and set aside.

- Heat the oil in a non-stick *kadai* and deep-fry the squares, a few at a time, till golden brown. Drain on absorbent paper.
- Place the fried potato squares on individual serving plates, drizzle with the chilli-garlic chutney and date and tamarind chutney, sprinkle *chaat masala* and serve immediately.

Dal Samosa

¾ cup skinless split green gram

½ cup refined flour

2 green chillies

3 cloves

2 teaspoons fennel seeds

4-5 black peppercorns

1 inch ginger, chopped

4 tablespoons ghee

A generous pinch of asafoetida

½ teaspoon cumin seeds

½ teaspoon red chilli powder

Salt to taste

2 teaspoons *chaat masala*

Oil for deep-frying

- Soak the green gram in three cups of water for two hours. Drain and grind coarsely using very little water.
- Grind together the green chillies, cloves, fennel seeds, peppercorns and ginger to a paste.
- Heat two tablespoons of ghee in a non-stick *kadai*; add the asafoetida and cumin seeds. When the seeds begin to change colour, add the chilli powder and gram paste.

Dal Samosa

- Sauté for three or four minutes and add the green chilli paste and salt.
- Cover the pan and cook till the gram is soft. Sprinkle a little water occasionally to prevent scorching. Add the *chaat masala* and mix well. Remove from heat and set aside to cool. Divide into eight portions.
- Sift the refined flour with a little salt. Rub in two tablespoons of the hot ghee. Add enough water and knead to make a stiff dough. Divide into four portions and roll each one out into a thin oval shaped *chapati*. Cut in half and fold into a cone. Fill with a portion of the green gram mixture and seal the open edges.
- Heat sufficient oil in a non-stick *kadai* and deep-fry the *samose* on medium heat till golden brown and crisp. Drain on absorbent paper.
- Serve hot with Green Chutney (page 93).

Vegetable Frankies

1 medium carrot, grated

¼ cup green peas, parboiled and crushed

2 large potatoes, boiled and mashed

4 refined flour *roti*

1 tablespoon oil + for shallow-frying

½ teaspoon cumin seeds

½ inch ginger, finely chopped

1 green chilli, finely chopped

¼ teaspoon red chilli powder

A pinch of turmeric powder

¼ teaspoon *garam masala* powder

Salt to taste

1 tablespoon chopped fresh coriander

½ teaspoon dried mango powder

To Serve

4 teaspoons Green Chutney (page 93)

1 medium onion, sliced

1 teaspoon vinegar

Chaat masala to taste

- Heat the oil in a non-stick pan; add the cumin seeds and sauté lightly. Add the carrot, green peas, ginger, green chilli, chilli powder, turmeric powder, *garam masala* powder and salt, and sauté over medium heat for two minutes. Transfer to a plate to cool.
- Add the mashed potatoes, chopped coriander and dried mango powder and mix well. Adjust the seasoning.
- Divide the potato mixture into eight portions and shape into four-inch long rolls. Shallow-fry in hot oil till light golden. Drain on absorbent paper and set aside.

- To prepare each frankie, place a *roti* on a flat working surface, spread a teaspoon of green chutney all over the *roti*. Place a potato roll on one side. Sprinkle some sliced onions, drizzle one-fourth teaspoon of vinegar, sprinkle *chaat masala* over and roll up the *roti*.
- Wrap in aluminum foil and serve immediately.

Masala Sandwich Double Roti Chaat

8 *pav*

4 medium potatoes, boiled and mashed

2 teaspoons oil

½ teaspoon mustard seeds

1 teaspoon red chilli powder

¼ teaspoon turmeric powder

½ teaspoon *garam masala* powder

Salt to taste

3-4 tablespoons butter

4 tablespoons Green Chutney (page 93)

4 tablespoons Date and Tamarind Chutney (page 93)

1 medium onion, chopped

8 tablespoons *sev*

4 tablespoons chopped fresh coriander

- Heat the oil in a non-stick pan; add the mustard seeds and when they begin to splutter, add the mashed potatoes, chilli powder, turmeric powder, *garam masala* powder and salt. Mix well and cook for three or four minutes. Remove and set aside.

Masala Sandwich Double Roti Chaat

- Slit two *pav* horizontally, but do not cut through to separate the halves. Spread some butter on the insides of the *pav*. Stuff with the potato mixture and lightly toast the *pav* on a *tawa* using a little butter.
- Arrange the two roasted *pav* on each serving plate. Top with the green chutney, date and tamarind chutney, onion and a generous helping of *sev*.
- Garnish with chopped coriander and serve immediately.

Grilled Corn And Capsicum Toasties

8 slices white bread
1 cup sweet corn kernels, boiled
1 medium green capsicum, chopped
1½ cups grated processed cheese
2-3 green chillies, chopped
2 tablespoons chopped fresh coriander
1 medium onion, chopped
7-8 black peppercorns, crushed
Salt to taste
Tomato ketchup, to serve

- Preheat an oven to 180°C/350°F/Gas Mark 4.
- In a bowl, mix the sweet corn, capsicum, cheese, green chillies, chopped coriander, onion, crushed peppercorns and salt. Divide the mixture into eight equal portions.
- Toast the slices of bread on one side on a non-stick tawa.
- Spread the corn and cheese mixture on the other side
- Place on a baking tray and bake till the topping turns golden brown.
- Cut each slice diagonally in half and serve hot with tomato ketchup.

Baked Bean Wraps

4 wholewheat *roti*

1½ cups tinned baked beans

2 medium onions

1 tablespoon oil

1 medium green capsicum, chopped

5-6 garlic cloves, thinly sliced

3 tablespoons chopped fresh coriander

Tomato ketchup, as required

Red chilli sauce, as required

A few iceberg lettuce leaves, shredded

4 tablespoons grated processed cheese

- Finely chop one onion and slice the other.
- Heat the oil in a non-stick pan; add the chopped onion, capsicum and garlic, and sauté for a few minutes.
- Add the baked beans and sauté for a while. Add the chopped coriander and mix.
- Place the *roti* on a flat surface. Spread a little tomato ketchup and red chilli sauce on each one.
- Place some of the baked bean mixture at one end of each *roti*. Sprinkle the sliced onion, lettuce and grated cheese over the baked beans and roll up tightly.
- Cut each roll into diagonal pieces and serve; or wrap each roll in aluminium foil and serve.

Bread Rolls

8 large slices of bread, crusts removed

1½ cups grated mozzarella cheese

1 medium onion, finely chopped

3 tablespoons chopped fresh coriander

1 green chilli, finely chopped

Salt to taste

Oil for deep-frying

To Serve

Mint Chutney (page 93)

- In a bowl, combine the mozzarella cheese, onion, chopped coriander, green chilli and salt.
- Soak the slices of bread, one at a time, in water for about ten seconds. Squeeze out the excess water by gently pressing between your palms.
- Place each slice on the worktop, place some of the cheese mixture at one end and roll the bread up firmly to cover the stuffing completely, ensuring that the edges are well sealed.
- Heat sufficient oil in a deep non-stick pan and deep-fry the rolls until golden brown. Drain on absorbent paper. Serve hot with tomato ketchup or mint chutney.

Bread Rolls

Cajun Vegetable Pizza

Pizza Base

1½ cups refined flour

1½ teaspoon dried yeast

1 teaspoon sugar

1 teaspoon salt

1 tablespoon oil + for greasing

Sauce

2 tablespoons olive oil

1 small onion, chopped

4-5 garlic cloves, chopped

4 medium tomatoes, finely chopped

A few leaves of fresh basil, torn into small pieces

Salt to taste

1 teaspoon crushed red chillies

Topping

1½ cups grated mozzarella cheese

¼ teaspoon dried oregano

4 tomatoes, seeded and cut into thin strips

2 medium onions, sliced

½ medium capsicum, cut into thin strips

½ cup sweetcorn kernels, boiled
1 tablespoon crushed red chillies
2 tablespoons olive oil
A few leaves of fresh basil, roughly torn

- For the pizza base, mix the yeast with a quarter cup of warm water and sugar, and set aside until frothy.
- Add the frothy yeast to the refined flour. Add the salt and one tablespoon oil, and mix. Add the water and knead into soft dough.
- Leave the dough covered with a damp cloth in a warm place for about forty-five minutes or until the dough has doubled in volume.
- Knead the dough again and set aside for ten to fifteen minutes, covered with a damp cloth.
- Preheat an oven to 220°C/425°F/Gas Mark 7.
- For the sauce, heat the olive oil in a non-stick pan; add the chopped onion and garlic, stir-fry briefly and add the tomatoes. Add one cup

of water and bring to a boil. Stir in the basil, salt and crushed chillies. Simmer for about five minutes on medium heat or till the sauce reaches a thick dropping consistency.

- Divide the pizza dough into four; roll out each portion into an eight-inch thick disc. Prick all over with a fork.
- Spread the prepared pizza sauce on the pizza bases. Sprinkle half a cup of the grated cheese and sprinkle the dried oregano. Place the pizza bases on a greased ovenproof tray and bake for eight to ten minutes, or until crisp.
- Remove from the oven and top it with the prepared vegetables. Sprinkle the crushed red chillies and the remaining grated cheese. Drizzle the olive oil and sprinkle the torn basil on top.
- Bake the pizza again for few minutes until the cheese melts and starts bubbling. Remove from the oven, cut each pizza into six or eight pieces and serve hot.

Cheesy Spinach Quesadillas

¼ cup grated processed cheese

700 grams spinach, blanched and chopped

1½ cups wholewheat flour

Salt to taste

3 tablespoons oil + for shallow-frying

2 garlic cloves, chopped

2 green chillies, finely chopped

½ teaspoon *garam masala* powder

- Mix the flour with salt and two tablespoons of oil. Add sufficient water and knead to make a soft dough. Divide into four portions and roll out each portion into a thin *chapati*. Heat a non-stick *tawa*, roast the *chapati* lightly and set aside.
- For the filling, heat one tablespoon of oil in a non-stick pan. Add the garlic and sauté for a minute. Add the spinach, green chillies, salt and *garam masala* powder, and mix well.
- Heat each *chapati* on a non-stick *tawa*. Spread half the spinach mixture over it and top with half the cheese. Place another *chapati* on

top. Drizzle a little oil all around and cook for a few minutes. Flip over and drizzle a little more oil all around. Cook till both sides are evenly golden brown and crisp.

- Cut into wedges and serve hot.

Cheesy Spinach Quesadillas

Corn And Vegetable Lollipops

½ cup fresh corn kernels, crushed
16 pieces baby corn
1 medium carrot, finely chopped
¼ cup shelled green peas, crushed
2 large potatoes, boiled and mashed
1 tablespoon oil + for deep-frying
Salt to taste
1 inch ginger, chopped
4-6 garlic cloves, chopped
2-3 green chillies, chopped
1 medium onion, chopped
1 tablespoon chopped fresh coriander
½ tablespoon light soy sauce
½ teaspoon white pepper powder
2 tablespoons cornflour
¼ cup refined flour

- Heat one tablespoon of oil in a non-stick pan. Add the carrot and peas, and sauté for a few seconds. Add the crushed corn and salt, and cook till the vegetables soften slightly.

- Place the mashed potatoes in a bowl; add the sautéed vegetables, ginger, garlic, green chillies, onion, chopped coriander, soy sauce, white pepper powder, salt and cornflour. Mix thoroughly.
- Divide the mixture into sixteen equal portions. Roll each portion into a ball and insert the thicker end of the baby corn into the ball. Press the mixture lightly between your palms to secure the baby corn.
- Heat the oil in a non-stick wok; roll the lollipops in the refined flour and shake to remove excess flour. Deep-fry over medium heat for three to four minutes, or till crisp and golden brown, turning occasionally. Drain on absorbent paper.
- Serve hot with Sichuan Sauce (page 94).

Garden Wraps

1 cup shredded iceberg lettuce

1 medium onion, sliced

2 medium cucumbers cut into thin strips

2 medium tomatoes cut into thin strips

½ cup bean sprouts

4 refined flour tortillas

½ cup cream cheese

1 teaspoon red chilli flakes

Salt to taste

- Spread the cream cheese on the tortillas.
- Top with the lettuce, onion, cucumbers, tomatoes and bean sprouts. Sprinkle the chilli flakes and salt on top.
- Roll up each tortilla tightly. Cut in half and serve immediately.

Chef's Tip

Replace the plain tortillas with tomato or other flavoured tortillas.

Garden Wraps

Fried Idli With Sichuan Sauce

10-12 *idli,* cut into fingers

1 tablespoon Sichuan Sauce (page 94)

2 tablespoons oil + for deep-frying

6 garlic cloves, chopped

4 spring onions, sliced

2 tablespoons tomato ketchup

3 spring onion green stalks, sliced

- Heat sufficient oil in a non-stick *kadai* and deep-fry the *idli* fingers till golden and crisp. Drain on absorbent paper.
- Heat two tablespoons of the oil in another non-stick *kadai*; add the garlic and sauté for half a minute. Add the spring onions and continue to sauté for another minute.
- Add the Sichuan sauce and tomato ketchup, and stir to mix. Add the fried *idli* and sauté over medium heat for one minute, tossing and stirring continuously.
- Add the spring onion greens and toss again to mix well.
- Serve hot.

Mini Falafel Burgers

1 cup chickpeas, soaked overnight

2-3 garlic cloves, chopped

2 tablespoons chopped fresh coriander

2 tablespoons chopped fresh parsley

4-5 spring onion green stalks, chopped

¼ cup breadcrumbs

A small pinch of soda bicarbonate

½ teaspoon roasted cumin powder

Salt to taste

¼ teaspoon black pepper powder

½ teaspoon *paprika*

Oil for deep-frying

Yogurt Sauce

½ cup drained (hung) yogurt

2 tablespoons cream

1 tablespoon chopped fresh coriander

3-4 garlic cloves, chopped

1 teaspoon chopped fresh parsley

Salt to taste

½ tablespoon lemon juice

To Serve

8 mini burger buns

Butter, as required

1 medium unpeeled cucumber, sliced into ribbons

Salt to taste

4 lettuce leaves, halved

2 processed cheese slices, quartered

1 medium cucumber, sliced

1 large tomato, sliced

- Drain the chickpeas and spread on a kitchen towel to dry. Process the chickpeas along with the garlic, chopped coriander, parsley, spring onion greens and breadcrumbs in a food processor to a coarse mixture.
- Add the soda bicarbonate and cumin powder, and mix well. Season with salt, pepper and *paprika*. Knead the mixture well and place in a refrigerator to chill for a couple of hours.
- Shape tablespoonfuls of the chilled mixture into round patties with the help of two wet tablespoons. Arrange on a greased plate and place in a refrigerator till ready to fry.
- Heat plenty of oil in a non-stick *kadai* and deep-fry the falafels till golden brown. Drain on absorbent paper.
- Mix together all the ingredients for the yogurt sauce and chill till required.
- Apply salt to the cucumber ribbons and set aside.
- Cut the burger buns into half and spread the cut sides with butter.

- On the bottom half of each bun place a lettuce leaf, a quartered cheese slice, cucumber slice and tomato slice.
- Place a fried falafel on the vegetable slices and top with the yogurt sauce and cucumber ribbons. Cover with the top half of the bun.
- Serve immediately.

Chef's Tip

In place of the mini burger buns you can also use small round buns.

Paneer And Capsicum Footlongs

250 grams cottage cheese, cut into 1-inch wide strips

1 small red capsicum

1 small yellow capsicum

1 small green capsicum

2 six-inch footlong loaves

2 tablespoons olive oil

3 garlic cloves, chopped

Salt to taste

2 jalapeño chillies, cut into thin strips

8-10 black peppercorns, crushed

2 tablespoons butter

2 teaspoons English mustard

4 large lettuce leaves

2 processed cheese slices, cut into triangles

6-8 fresh basil leaves, roughly torn

- Rub a little olive oil over the capsicums. Thread them onto a skewer or pierce with a fork and roast them, one by one, over a moderately hot open flame till charred. Plunge the roasted capsicums into cold water immediately. Peel, remove seeds and cut into thin strips.

- Heat two tablespoons of olive oil in a non-stick pan; add the garlic and sauté for half a minute. Add the cottage cheese strips, roasted capsicum strips, salt, jalapeño chillies and crushed peppercorns; cook for two minutes tossing and stirring continuously. Transfer to a plate and set aside to cool.
- To assemble the footlong, place one footlong on a board and slice it in half with a serrated knife. Butter one half of the loaf and spread English mustard on the other half.
- Place two lettuce leaves on the buttered side, topped with two cheese triangles, followed by a generous portion of the cottage cheese and capsicum mixture. Sprinkle with the torn basil leaves. Cover with the second half of the loaf. Wrap the sandwich in aluminium foil or a paper napkin and serve immediately.

Paneer and Capsicum Footlongs

Sesame Hot Noodles

2 tablespoons toasted sesame seeds

2 tablespoons sesame oil

400 grams eggless noodles

4 tablespoons oil

3-4 garlic cloves, chopped

2 spring onion bulbs, sliced

2 green chillies, chopped

3 tablespoons light soy sauce

1 tablespoon chilli sauce, or to taste

½ teaspoon white pepper powder

Salt to taste

½ cup peanuts, roasted and crushed

1 cup bean sprouts

1 tablespoon vinegar

- Boil the noodles in plenty of water till just done. Drain and mix in the sesame oil.
- Heat the oil in a non-stick wok. Add the garlic, spring onions and green chillies, and stir-fry for a few seconds. Add the noodles, soy sauce, chilli sauce, white pepper powder and salt, and continue to stir-fry for a couple of minutes.

- Add the peanuts, sesame seeds, bean sprouts and vinegar, and cook over a high heat for a minute, stirring and tossing continuously.
- Serve hot.

Chef's Tip

You can reduce the amount of chillies and chilli sauce for younger children and increase it if your older kids can take the heat!

Pizza Margherita

2 six-inch Pizza Bases (see below)

Sauce

2 cups Tomato Concassé (page 94)
½ cup tomato purée
1 tablespoon olive oil
2 garlic cloves, chopped
1 large pinch of dried oregano
1 small onion, chopped
2 fresh basil leaves, roughly torn
Salt to taste
½ teaspoon sugar
3-4 black peppercorns, crushed

Topping

1 cup grated mozzarella cheese
1 medium tomato, cut into round slices
4-5 fresh basil leaves
Salt to taste
3-4 black peppercorns, crushed
Dried oregano to taste

- For the sauce, heat the olive oil in a non-stick pan; add the garlic and the dried oregano, and sauté for half a minute. Add the onion and sauté till translucent.

Pizza Margherita

- Add the tomato concassé and mix till all the moisture has evaporated. Add the tomato purée and cook for another five to eight minutes.
- Add the roughly torn basil, salt, sugar, and the crushed peppercorns, and mix well. Set aside to cool.
- Preheat an oven to 200°C/400°F/Gas Mark 6.
- Spread the sauce evenly over both pizza bases and sprinkle with mozzarella cheese. Arrange the tomato slices and basil leaves on top and sprinkle with salt, crushed peppercorns and dried oregano to taste.
- Place the pizzas on a baking tray and bake for ten to fifteen minutes, till the cheese melts.
- Remove from the oven, cut into wedges and serve immediately.

Chef's Tip

Bake pizzas made with ready-made pizza bases, for ten to fifteen minutes. If using fresh pizza dough, bake for forty to forty-five minutes.

Pizza Base

1½ cups refined flour

1½ teaspoons dried yeast

1 teaspoon sugar

1 teaspoon salt

1 tablespoon oil

- Heat one-fourth cup of water till warm. Mix yeast with warm water and sugar in a bowl and set aside until frothy.
- Add the yeast mixture to the refined flour. Add salt and oil and mix well. Add approximately half a cup of water and knead into a soft dough.
- Cover the dough with a damp cloth and leave to rest in a warm place for about forty-five minutes, or until the dough is approximately double in size.
- Knead the dough again, cover with a damp cloth, and leave to stand for ten to fifteen minutes. Preheat the oven to 200°C/400°F/Gas Mark 6. Grease a baking tray.
- Divide pizza dough into two portions. Roll out each portion into six-inch rounds. Prick all over with a fork. Place the pizza bases on the baking tray and bake for eight minutes.

Singapore Noodles

200 grams rice noodles
Salt to taste
1 tablespoon oil
4 tablespoons Chilli Oil (page 93), or to taste
1 inch ginger, chopped
3-4 garlic cloves, chopped
¼ small cabbage, finely shredded
1 small carrot, grated
1 medium green capsicum, cut into thin strips
2 spring onions with greens, sliced
½ tablespoon light soy sauce
3 tablespoons tomato sauce
½ teaspoon white pepper powder
½ cup bean sprouts
1 tablespoon white vinegar

- Boil six cups of water in a deep non-stick pan. Add the salt and one tablespoon of oil. Add the noodles; take the pan off the heat, cover and leave to stand for three minutes. Drain the noodles, refresh in cold water and drain again. Spread on a large plate to cool.

- Heat the chilli oil in a non-stick wok; add the ginger and garlic, and stir-fry for one minute. Add the cabbage, carrot and capsicum, and continue to stir-fry for one minute. Add the spring onions, reserving some greens for garnishing, and cook on high heat for one minute more.
- Add the noodles, soy sauce, tomato sauce, white pepper powder and salt to taste. Mix well and cook for a couple of minutes, tossing and stirring continuously.
- Add the bean sprouts and vinegar, and toss well. Serve hot, garnished with reserved spring onion greens.

Chef's Tip

You can replace some of the chilli oil with vegetable oil for a milder version.

Cheesy Macaroni

1 cup grated processed cheese

300 grams macaroni, boiled

6 tablespoons butter

2 tablespoons refined flour

2 cups milk

Salt to taste

White pepper powder to taste

2 tablespoons fresh breadcrumbs

½ teaspoon crushed black peppercorns

½ tablespoon chopped fresh parsley

- Preheat an oven to 220°C/425°F/Gas Mark 7.
- Heat two tablespoons of the butter in a non-stick frying pan; add the flour and sauté lightly, making sure that it does not change colour.
- Gradually add the milk, stirring continuously, so that no lumps form.
- Add half the grated cheese and continue to stir. After adding the cheese, the sauce will thicken further, so add more milk to adjust the consistency.

Cheesy Macaroni

- Add the salt and white pepper powder, and mix well.
- Heat two tablespoons of butter in a separate non-stick pan. Add the macaroni and toss to mix. Strain the sauce into the pan and mix gently.
- Add the remaining cheese and transfer the mixture into a seven-inch square baking dish. Sprinkle the breadcrumbs over the top and dot with the remaining butter. Sprinkle the crushed peppercorns and parsley. Bake till the cheese melts and turns golden. Serve hot.

Mini Tostadas

12 ready-made corn tostadas

A few iceberg lettuce leaves, torn into bite-sized pieces

1 tablespoon pomegranate kernels

A few sprigs of fresh parsley

Salsa

½ cup corn kernels

1 tablespoon olive oil

1 medium onion, chopped

1 medium green capsicum, cut into small pieces

1 medium red capsicum, cut into small pieces

1 medium yellow capsicum, cut into small pieces

50 grams cottage cheese, cut into small pieces

7-8 black peppercorns, crushed

¼ teaspoon paprika

1 tablespoon chopped fresh coriander

Salt to taste

1 tablespoon lemon juice

1 tablespoon balsamic vinegar (optional)

- For the salsa, roast the corn in a non-stick pan over high heat to scorch the kernels lightly. Add the olive oil and onion, and sauté till translucent. Remove from heat and transfer to a bowl. Set aside to cool.
- Place the capsicums and cottage cheese in a separate bowl. Add the crushed peppercorns, *paprika*, chopped coriander, salt and lemon juice, and mix well.
- Add the sautéed corn, onions and balsamic vinegar. Adjust salt and toss to mix.
- To assemble, place the lettuce leaf on a plate and place a piece of lettuce leaf on each. Spoon some salsa on each tostada.
- Garnish with pomegranate kernels and parsley sprigs, and serve immediately.

Chef's Tip

Ready-made tostadas are easily available in the market.

Mini Tostadas

Secret Noodles

2 packets instant noodles with seasoning

1 medium carrot, cut into small cubes

1 medium tomato, puréed

50 grams processed cheese, cut into ½-inch cubes

¼ cup shelled green peas, blanched

Salt to taste

Toothpicks as required

- Heat three cups of water in a non-stick pan; add the noodles, carrot, half the green peas and the seasoning, and bring to a boil.
- Add the tomato purée and salt if required, and cook until the noodles are tender and the moisture has been absorbed.
- Thread the cheese cubes and remaining green peas alternately onto toothpicks.
- Serve the noodles in deep bowls garnished with the cheese-n-pea toothpicks.

Herb And Garlic Bread

1 tablespoon dried oregano

10-12 garlic cloves, finely chopped

1 French loaf

100 grams butter

- Preheat an oven to 200°C/400°F/ Gas Mark 6.
- Soften the butter, add the oregano and garlic, and mix well.
- Cut the loaf into one-inch thick slices without cutting through. Spread the garlic butter generously between the slices. Wrap the loaf in aluminium foil and bake for fifteen minutes.
- Separate the slices and serve warm.

Peanut Raisin Bars

1 cup peanuts, roasted and crushed

¾ cup seedless raisins

¼ cup butter + for greasing

¼ cup sugar

¼ cup honey

1½ cups cornflakes

- Grease a tray.
- Heat the butter in a non-stick pan. Add the sugar and honey. Mix and simmer for three minutes. Remove from heat.
- Stir in the raisins, crushed peanuts and cornflakes.
- Spread in the greased tray and press firmly with a flat spoon.
- Mark into bars with a knife while still warm.
- When cool, cut through and separate the pieces.
- Store in an airtight container.

Kela Halwa

2 cups ripe Rajali banana pulp

1 cup sugar

4 tablespoons pure ghee
+ for greasing

- Cook the banana pulp and sugar together in a thick-bottomed non-stick pan, stirring continuously, till the mixture starts to thicken.
- Add two tablespoons of ghee and continue to cook, stirring continuously. As it thickens some more, add the rest of the ghee and continue to cook stirring all the while.
- To check if cooked, roll a small quantity with your palms into a ball, if it does not stick it is ready.
- Pour the mixture onto a greased *thali* and spread evenly with a greased rolling pin or the back of a flat spoon.
- Cut into square or diamond-shaped pieces while still hot, but do not separate the pieces. Set aside to cool; separate the pieces and store.

Note: If Rajali bananas are not available, you can use the ripe green plantains.

Kela Halwa

Khajoori Shahi Tukre

1 cup seedless dates, finely chopped

8 slices bread

5 cups milk

Ghee for shallow-frying

10-12 pistachios

8-10 almonds

½ teaspoon green cardamom powder

½ cup sugar

Edible silver foil to garnish

½ teaspoon rose water

- Trim the crust and cut each slice of bread into round shapes with a cookie cutter or a *katori*. Heat the ghee in a non-stick pan and shallow-fry the bread rounds for about a minute. Turn over and fry for about a minute longer, or until light brown and crisp. Drain on absorbent paper.
- Soak the pistachios and almonds in hot water for ten minutes. Drain, peel and slice. Reserve one tablespoon of sliced pistachios and almonds for garnishing.

- Mix together the dates and cardamom powder, and mash thoroughly with a rolling pin. Add the sliced pistachios and almonds, and mix well. Divide the mixture into four equal portions.
- Place a portion of the date mixture on a fried bread round, cover with another round and press down to enclose the filling.
- Meanwhile, bring the milk to boil, lower the heat and simmer, stirring continuously, for ten minutes, or until the quantity is reduced by half. Add the sugar and continue to simmer for five minutes, stirring continuously.
- Dip the stuffed bread rounds into the thick sweetened milk for half a minute, remove and set aside. Cook the remaining milk for five to six minutes, stirring continuously or until it thickens to a coating consistency. Remove from heat and chill.
- Place the soaked bread pieces on a serving dish, pour the chilled reduced milk on top, cover with the edible silver foil and top with the reserved pistachios and almonds. Serve, sprinkled with the rose water.

Microwaved Eggless Chocolate Cake

100 grams dark cooking chocolate, grated
1 cup butter, cut into cubes
1⅓ cups refined flour
2 teaspoons baking powder
1 cup + 2 tablespoons powdered sugar
1 teaspoon vanilla essence
¾ cup milk
½ cup chopped walnut kernels
Butter for greasing

- Grease a microwave-safe dish.
- Melt the chocolate and butter in a microwave-safe bowl in the microwave oven for one minute on HIGH (100%).
- In a separate bowl, sift the refined flour and baking powder.
- Mix the melted butter and chocolate well. Stir in the powdered sugar and vanilla essence.
- Fold in the sifted flour and baking powder. Adjust the consistency by adding milk and gently fold in the walnuts.
- Pour the batter into the greased dish. Bake on HIGH (100%) for seven minutes. Leave to stand for five minutes. Cool, cut into slices and serve.

Annexure

- ***Chilli Oil***

  Cook 6 tablespoons of chopped dried red chillies in 1¼ cups of groundnut oil on low heat for at least ten minutes. When completely cold, stir in 2-3 tablespoons of red chilli powder and 1-2 tablespoons of sesame oil. Cover and leave to stand for at least twelve hours. Strain into a sterilised bottle and store in a cool, dark place.

- ***Date And Tamarind Chutney***

  Wash, stone and chop 15-20 dates. Dry-roast 2 teaspoons cumin seeds and ¼ teaspoon fennel seeds. Cool and grind to a powder. Cook the dates, 1 cup tamarind pulp, cumin and fennel powder, ½ cup jaggery, 2 teaspoons red chilli powder, 1 teaspoon dried ginger powder, black salt, salt and four cups of water till thick.

- ***Green Chutney***

  Grind together 1 cup fresh coriander, ½ cup fresh mint, 2-3 green chillies, black salt to taste, ¼ teaspoon sugar and 1 tablespoon lemon juice to a smooth paste using a little water if required.

- ***Mint Chutney***

  Grind 5 cups mint leaves, 3 cups coriander leaves, 10 green chillies, 3 onions, and 3 inches of ginger to a fine paste, adding a little water if required. Stir in 1 tablespoon lemon juice, salt and pomegranate seed powder to taste.

- ***Red Chilli-Garlic Chutney***

  Soak 10 red chillies in 1½ cups of water for half an hour. Drain and grind with 12 large garlic cloves and 2 teaspoons lemon juice to a fine paste. Add sea salt and 1 teaspoon cumin powder and mix well.

- ***Sichuan Sauce***

  Boil 10-12 dried red chillies in 1 cup of water for 5 to 7 minutes. Drain, cool and grind to a fine paste. Heat ½ cup oil in a pan; add 10 finely chopped garlic cloves, 2 finely chopped green chillies, 2 finely chopped spring onions and 1 inch ginger, grated, and sauté for 1 minute. Add the red chilli paste and sauté for a few more seconds. Add 2-3 inches celery stalk, finely chopped, 3 tablespoons tomato ketchup and salt to taste, and stir well to mix. Stir in 2 teaspoons white vinegar and simmer for 1 minute till the oil rises to the surface. Cool and store.

  Note: Sichuan sauce will keep for 1 month if there is sufficient oil covering the surface.

- ***Tomato Concassé***

  To make 1 cup of tomato concassé, blanch 5 medium tomatoes in plenty of boiling water for two minutes. Drain and refresh in cold water; peel, cut in half, remove seeds and chop roughly.